Shortcuts

A CONCISE GUIDE TO ROTARY CUTTING

Donna Lynn Thomas

Desert Storm Hearts. One went, one stayed but both are missing a piece. The author and her husband each wore one for the duration of Desert Storm. Reunited, their hearts are again whole.

Credits

Photography . . . . Brent Kane
Illustration . . . . Linda and
                 Chris Gentry of Artworks
Text and Cover Design . . Judy Petry
Editor . . . . Liz McGehee

Dedication

This book is dedicated to my beloved husband, Terry, whose return is awaited with joy and open arms. One day soon he will be home and the missing piece will be back in place to make my heart whole again.

Acknowledgments

First, I'd like to thank Nancy Martin for letting me use photos of quilts from her collection.

On a personal level, I'd like to give a heartfelt thank-you to Marion Shelton, Nancy Martin, and the staff at That Patchwork Place, for their warmth, genuine concern, and understanding as I worked on *Shortcuts* during stressful times. This book served as a day-to-day anchor for me, but I couldn't have done it without their supportive phone calls and the sense that they really cared. They touched my heart and reconfirmed my belief that quilters are truly special people.

I would like to thank Judy Martin for generously allowing me to use her original block design "Land of the Midnight Sun" from her book, *Judy Martin's Ultimate Book of Quilt Block Patterns*.

Front Cover Quilt: *The Sawtooth Star quilt designed by Marsha McCloskey was pieced by Emily Nelson and Julie Peterzelka of Calico Creations, Mount Vernon, Washington. (Collection of Nancy J. Martin)*

Shortcuts: A Concise Guide to Rotary Cutting©
©1991 by Donna Lynn Thomas

That Patchwork Place, Inc.
PO Box 118, Bothell, WA 98041-0118

Printed in the United States of America
96 95 94 93   6

Library of Congress Cataloging-in-Publication Data

Thomas, Donna Lynn
    Shortcuts : a concise guide to rotary cutting / by Donna Lynn Thomas.
      p.   cm.
     ISBN 0-943574-87-0
     1. Patchwork.   2. Cutting.   I. Title.
TT835.T45   1991
746.9'7—dc20   91-4275
                                              CIP

Contents

 *Introduction*

It is human nature to constantly seek out new ways and new tools to accomplish a task. It is this quality in man that took us from caves into organized agriculture and society, and on into our modern world. Of course, on a much humbler level, it has resulted in a revolution in the world of quiltmaking. Innovations along the way, such as marked sewing lines, layered cutting, the introduction of plastic for templates, and a myriad of "tricks-of-the-trade," have made the job easier.

Somewhere, not too long ago, some ingenious mind devised the concept of quick piecing, that is, the idea of sewing strips of fabric together first and cutting them into segments to save time and avoid tedious marking and cutting. Someone also thought of using an office paper cutter to quickly cut quantities of strips. The idea was hot; quilters began seeing the tremendous possibilities, and they set their minds to work on it. What followed was an avalanche of ideas and techniques for quick piecing quilts. Somewhere in the midst of this arose the rotary cutter and ruler, tools for accurately quick cutting. Consequently, they became the perfect companions for quick piecing. The restless quilter's mind is still at work and the innovations continue.

There are some who dismiss these modern techniques, feeling they take away from the primary pleasures of quiltmaking. This may be true for some, but generally there is a place for both the old and new in our lives. Even though most of my cutting and piecing is done by machine, I still need the quiet, retrospective time found only by hand piecing and hand quilting—there is always a "by hand" project in my quilt basket. On the other hand, there are times when I can't wait to see an idea come together and still other times when rotary cutting and fast piecing are the only techniques that provide me with the ability and accuracy needed to make the quilt. A good example of this are the tiny miniature quilts I dearly love to make.

Shortcuts compiles these basic quick-cutting techniques into one working book. In addition to what have become the standards of rotary cutting, I have included a number of techniques that are expansions of the basics. They are intended not only to inform you but also to get your mental juices flowing with other possibilities. As you explore these methods, you most likely will discover some shortcuts of your own.

General Information

One of the first things you'll notice about rotary cutting is the absence of a marked sewing line on the fabric. Seam allowances (the traditional ¼" on each side) are included in the dimensions of the pieces when cut. Be sure to remember this when working with patterns and books geared specifically toward rotary cutting. It is even more important to remember to add the seam allowances to your figuring when preparing to adapt your own patterns for rotary cutting. *Shortcuts* provides you with all the information you need to properly figure what size to cut your pieces to obtain the desired finished size.

Generally, the use of a rotary cutter precludes the use of hard templates, although you will find as you read *Shortcuts* that there are instances where you do use paper cutting guides attached to the ruler to accurately quick-cut shapes with odd sizes or angles. Once you make your cutting guide, the method is quick and accurate compared to individual hand marking.

With the discussion of each geometric shape, you will find a sample block using that shape and also an icon identifying that shape. Icons are a quick visual means of identifying what needs to be cut for a particular pattern without lengthy descriptions. I use them extensively when developing my own patterns—they are like a quilter's shorthand. Icons are used in the last section of this book to help show how several block patterns can be adapted to rotary cutting.

All the accurate cutting methods in the world won't mean a thing if your sewing is not accurate. Be careful to sew an accurate ¼" seam allowance. A good first step is to check the accuracy of your machine's ¼" guide by conducting a strip test. Cut three 1½" x 3" strips and seam them together side by side. When sewn, the center strip should measure exactly 1". If not, try shifting your machine needle one notch to the right, or mark a new masking-tape guide on the throat plate of your machine.

Icon

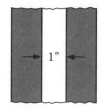

After you sew the three 1½" strips together side by side, center strip should measure a perfect 1" from seam to seam.

Align the ¼" mark on a piece of graph paper just to the left of the needle. Put the unthreaded needle into the paper just to the right of the ¼" grid line so the needle is included in the ¼" area.

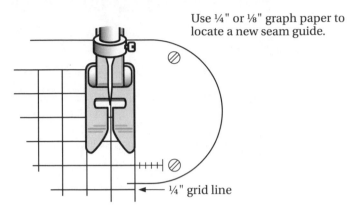

Use ¼" or ⅛" graph paper to locate a new seam guide.

← ¼" grid line

Place a masking-tape guide on the throat plate along the right edge of the graph paper. Adjust the guide so that it runs straight down from the needle and is not canted to either the left or right.

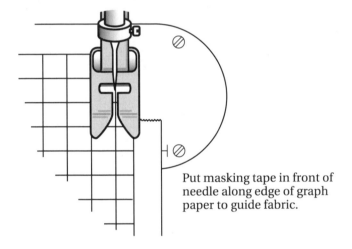

Put masking tape in front of needle along edge of graph paper to guide fabric.

Cut a new set of strips and try the strip test again with the new guide. Keep adjusting and testing the guide until you can produce a perfect 1" strip every time. Once you have the proper mark, build up several layers of tape or fasten a piece of adhesive-backed moleskin on the right side of this mark to better guide the fabric edge.

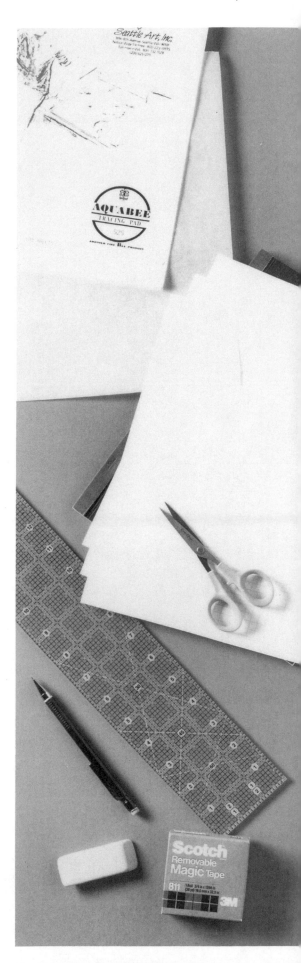

Equipment

Many books and patterns are available today with instructions specifically geared toward rotary cutting. Listed below are the supplies and equipment you will need to adapt your own pattern ideas to rotary-cutting specifications.

BASIC SUPPLIES

Graph paper: Every design begins with a drawing, whether full-size or to scale. It is important to have accurate ⅛"-grid graph paper on hand for your drawings. Some people like paper with the inch lines highlighted, but it is not necessary.

Lead pencil: I prefer a fine-point mechanical pencil, but a well-sharpened, #2 lead pencil and sharpener works equally well.

Eraser: Be sure to use a good-quality eraser for mistakes. An engineer's eraser does not damage the paper as easily as the basic school eraser does.

Tracing paper: Tracing paper is used for making paper cutting guides that are taped to your rotary ruler for cutting certain shapes.

Transparent tape: You need removable tape for your tracing paper or it will become torn.

Drafting ruler: I use my 3" x 18" rotary ruler for drafting, not only because it has all the markings I like but also because its angle markings are so helpful in drafting diamonds, triangles, and other geometric shapes.

Scissors: Use a pair of sharp paper scissors for cutting your paper cutting guides.

ROTARY EQUIPMENT

Rotary Cutters

A rotary cutter is a round-bladed cutting instrument attached to a handle. It looks like a pizza cutter with a protective shield that is either manually or automatically released, depending on the model. Rotary cutters come in two different sizes—large and small. For full-size quilts, I prefer the larger

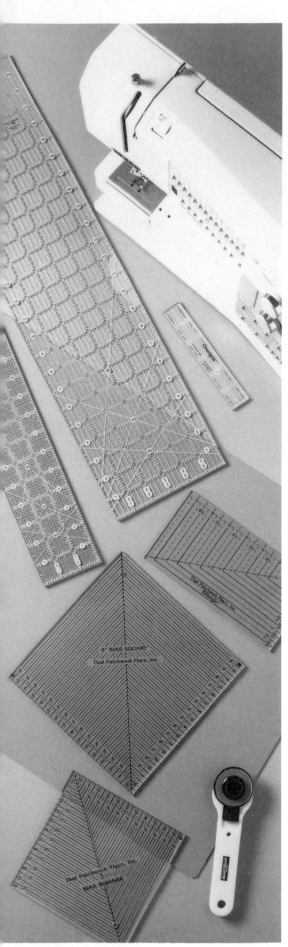

blade as it stays sharp longer, but when working with miniature or small quilts, the small cutter is more useful. Be sure to keep several replacement blades on hand. Periodically, the blade will become dull or nicked and must be replaced. It is also necessary to clean the lint from between the blade and the front sheath. Do this by dismantling the cutter, carefully wiping the blade clean with a soft, clean cloth, and adding a very small drop of sewing machine oil to the blade where it lies under the front sheath. You may find that your cutter feels like it has a new blade after this simple cleaning process.

Rotary blades are extremely sharp cutting instruments and must therefore be treated with a great deal of care to avoid accidents. Please keep these tools well out of the reach of children—they can easily sever tiny fingers. Before using a cutter with a manual safety shield, make it a practice of tightening the back screw so that the safety shield cannot be easily pushed back from the blade with simple pressure on the cutter. It is very important that you make it a conscious habit to engage the manual safety mechanism at the completion of every single cutting stroke. Even though the automatic safety shield is designed to "remember" for us, I prefer cutters with the manual safety shield. The automatics have a spring mechanism that automatically covers the blade when not in use and easily retracts when pressure is applied for cutting. In addition to the obvious dangers in the hands of children, these mechanisms also easily retract when dropped on adult feet or hands. I also find the automatic spring impedes cutting when working with several layers of fabric.

Another important safety precaution is to always cut away from your body. One slip or overly powerful stroke toward yourself could result in a painful cut on your thigh or elsewhere.

Rotary Mats

You must have a rotary mat to use with your rotary cutter. If you try to cut fabric on anything but a mat specifically made for rotary cutters, you will immediately ruin both your blade and the cutting surface.

I use a large mat with 1" grid lines on my work table and an 18" x 24" mat for workshops. Always store your mats flat and keep them away from extreme temperatures that can warp them irreparably. Keep hot items such as irons, coffee pots, and mugs off the mats for the same reason.

Rotary Rulers

A good rotary ruler is an invaluable tool and a necessity for rotary cutting. There are many types of rulers now available, ranging from highly specialized tools to general-purpose rulers. Look for the following features in choosing a rotary ruler.

Rotary rulers are made of clear, hard acrylic that is ⅛" thick. They come in all shapes and sizes with an assortment of markings. I find that a ruler with ⅛" markings is absolutely necessary. These ⅛" marks should appear on every inch line both horizontally and vertically. You will find a ruler with 30°, 45°, and 60° lines to be essential also. Of course, the corner of the ruler is the 90° guide. A "window" at the intersection of each inch line is also helpful in guaranteeing that the edge of your fabric is where it ought to be in relation to the markings.

Rulers that are 24" long are useful for cutting large strips and shapes, and for working with fabric folded selvage to selvage. These rulers are generally 6" wide, which is helpful when cutting wide border strips.

A 3" x 18" or 6" x 12" ruler is a nice size for most work as long as the fabric is folded twice—fold selvage to selvage and then fold again to selvages. I find the 3" x 18" to be the size I use most often, unless I need strips or shapes wider than 3", in which case I switch to the 6" x 12" or 6" x 24" size.

I keep a 1" x 6" ruler by my sewing machine to constantly check my work for accuracy. This ruler is definitely a must when working with small quilts or small pieces.

Although 6" x 24" rulers can be used to cut large squares in conjunction with the lines on the rotary mat, it is very helpful to have a large square ruler, such as a 15" x 15" size, to more easily achieve the same goal.

One other ruler that I would never be without is the Bias Square®. It comes in two sizes—6" x 6" and 8" x 8" in both linear and metric versions—and has ⅛" markings with a 45°-angle line running diagonally, corner to corner. Its main function is to cut presewn bias squares, but it serves many other useful purposes as you will learn later.

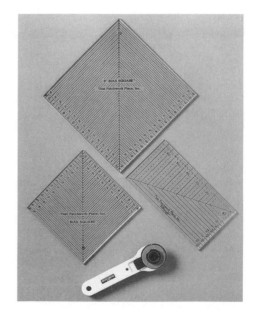

Until the Bias Square was introduced several years ago, the most advanced way to preassemble bias squares was to draw grid lines on two layers of fabric, sew the layers together on the lines, and then cut the grids apart. Unfortunately, this method had too many variables that increased the chances of inaccuracy with each step. The new bias-square method and the Bias Square® were exactly what was needed to enable quilters to construct highly accurate bias squares without frustration.

Since the degree of accuracy is considerably greater and more easily attained with this new method, I have used it to construct all my bias squares.

Last, but not least, if you plan on using pieced rectangles in any of your quilt designs, I urge you to consider purchasing Mary Hickey's BiRangle™ ruler. Her method for strip piecing and cutting presewn, pieced rectangles (pages 41–43) is a tremendous addition to any quilter's inventory of techniques.

Getting Ready

44"/45" wide

warp

weft

Warp yarns form the lengthwise grain. The warp yarns on either side form the fabric selvages after the weft yarns are woven in.

Weft yarns are woven back and forth through the warp yarns to form the crosswise grain.

FABRIC AND GRAIN LINE

It is helpful to understand the weaving process in order to understand why each type of grain has its own special properties. When fabric is woven on a hand loom, the process begins with the long warp yarns attached to the front bar of the loom. If ten yards of fabric are desired, then the warp yarns are cut ten yards long, plus enough extra yardage to roll the ends tightly onto the bar on the opposite end of the loom. There are as many yarns lined up across the front bar as are needed to make the fabric as wide as desired. When the fabric is finished, these warp yarns are referred to as the lengthwise grain of the fabric.

Once the warp yarns are secured in place on the loom, yarns are wound on a shuttle and woven back and forth from side to side through the warp yarns. These new side-to-side weft yarns are referred to as the crosswise grain of the finished fabric. The process, though simplified, is the same process used in modern, mechanized fabric production.

Lengthwise grain has little or no give. This is the result of the warp yarns being tightly secured at both ends during the weaving process. The lack of give means that edges cut parallel to this grain will not stretch with handling.

Crosswise grain has a slight amount of give, since the weft yarns are not secured to anything except the warp yarns when woven from side to side. Even so, the yarn itself will only give so far, depending on the quality of the yarn used. Edges cut parallel to the crosswise grain can stretch slightly if roughly handled. Cutting on either the lengthwise or crosswise grain is considered to be cutting on grain, unless a pattern specifically instructs you to cut on one type of grain instead of the other.

Bias is anything other than lengthwise or crosswise grain, although true bias is defined as the direction running at a 45° angle to the other grains. Think of the lengthwise and crosswise grains as forming a square. Bias runs from corner to corner across the diagonal of the square. It has a generous amount of give when pulled since there are no diagonal yarns restraining it. Be careful when handling edges cut parallel to the bias. They can easily become distorted, stretched, and wavy if pulled and overhandled.

Generally, when making quilts, we try to cut shapes as close to straight of grain (S-O-G) as possible. It's difficult to rotary cut strips that are true straight of grain, so we settle for "close" grain with satisfactory results. Due to the quirks of mass production, few fabrics are printed on grain, and many are stretched off grain when rolled onto bolts for sale. A piece of fabric that is badly off grain can sometimes be pulled straight by holding opposite diagonal corners and gently pulling.

All squares, strips, and rectangles should be cut on grain. Some shapes, such as triangles, cannot have all edges cut on grain. Therefore, it is a good idea to look at the position of the shape in the pattern and consider a few guidelines when deciding which edges should be cut on grain.

1. Place all edges on the perimeter of a quilt block on grain so the block does not stretch out of shape.
2. Whenever possible, without violating rule 1, sew a bias edge to a straight edge to stabilize the seam.

Note: The cutting directions in *Shortcuts* are based on the most common placement of grain line. You may need to make your own adjustments for certain grain situations.

FABRIC PREPARATION

There are many schools of thought on whether to prewash or not and, more specifically, on how to prewash. We each have our own preferences, and I advise you to follow what works for you. In the end, what is important for successful rotary cutting is that the fabric be pressed smooth with selvages together. If the fabric is slippery, apply a bit of spray sizing to help tame the edges so they don't slip while cutting. I like to steam the edges of cotton fabrics just before cutting to take advantage of cotton's natural self-adhesive quality.

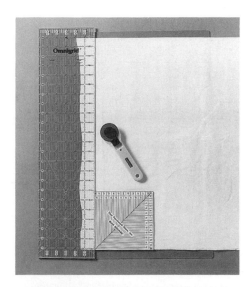

Preparing the Fabric Edges for Cutting

Lay the freshly pressed fabric on the rotary mat with the fold toward you, the raw edges to the left (reverse if left-handed), and the selvages at the top of the mat.

Place the edge of your rotary ruler inside the raw edge of the fabric. To make a cut at a right angle to the fold, lay one edge of the Bias Square® along the fold of the fabric and adjust the straight ruler so that it is flush with the Bias Square. Be sure to hold the ruler absolutely still with firm, downward pressure and fingers spread wide so the ruler doesn't shift. Some quilters find it helpful to anchor their ruler by placing their outer fingers or the palm of their hand to the left of the ruler.

Now, push the Bias Square out of the way. Retract the rotary cutter's safety mechanism, place the blade next to the ruler's edge, and begin to cut slowly away from yourself with firm, downward pressure. As the blade rolls along the ruler's edge, it may sometimes be necessary to slowly and carefully "walk" your hand up the ruler. Be careful not to shift the ruler out of line. Cut completely past the selvages and engage the safety mechanism again before putting the cutter back on the table. This newly cut edge is now your straight-of-grain cutting edge.

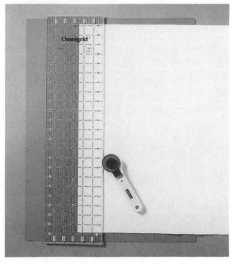

✎ Simple Cutting

STRIPS

Almost all rotary cutting begins with strips of fabric that are then cut into other shapes, such as squares, triangles, rectangles, and diamonds. Strips are cut with the straight-of-grain cut edge on the left. (Reverse these directions if you are left-handed.) The rest of the fabric lies to the right. Let's say you want to cut a 3" strip. Find the 3" line inside the right edge of your ruler and align that marking with the prepared left edge of the fabric. In addition, always have one of the ruler's horizontal lines even with the bottom edge of the fabric. If the cut is not at a right angle to the fold, you will end up with a "bent" strip. Strips are always cut ½" wider than the desired finished size to allow for the two side seams.

To cut a strip a particular length, line up the ruler to the proper length from the bottom at the same time you line up the width lines. A quick slice across the top of the ruler after completing the upward cut will yield a strip of specified length. In such a case, you would not extend your upward cut all the way past the selvages of the fabric.

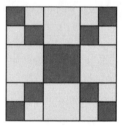

Ninepatch
Simple square: ☐

SQUARES

Squares are easily cut from strips. If 2" squares are needed for a Ninepatch block, for example, cut a 2" strip, turn the short end of the strip facing left, and start cutting 2" squares from the left to the right. Be sure to align a horizontal line of the ruler or Bias Square® across the bottom of the strip each time you prepare to cut. Squares and, consequently, the strips they are cut from are always cut ½" larger than the desired finished size to account for the seams.

The Bias Square is an excellent tool for cutting one or two squares. Lay the Bias Square at the lower left of the prepared fabric corner, with the appropriate marks on the fabric edges. A neat slice, up and across, yields the square.

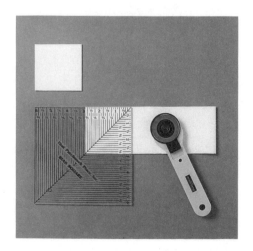

RIGHT TRIANGLES

There are two ways to cut right triangles for blocks, such as the Color Wheel block shown here. To determine the method you use, choose the edge on which the straight of grain should be placed. Both methods start with a square that is cut into either two or four triangles.

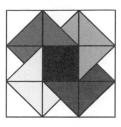

Color Wheel

Simple half-square triangle:

Simple quarter-square triangle:

Half-Square Triangles

This type of triangle is created by cutting a square in half on the diagonal to yield two triangles. In this case, the straight of grain is on the edges adjacent to the right-angle corner.

To compute the size square to cut, first determine the finished size of the short edge of the triangle. Add ⅞" to this figure and cut a square this size. Then, cut the square in half on the diagonal. Once all the seams are sewn, it will be the size you originally determined.

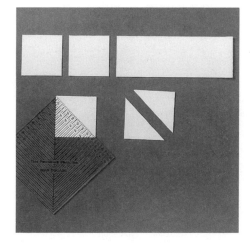

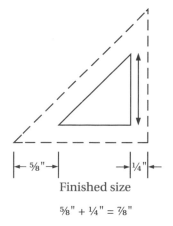

Finished size

⅝" + ¼" = ⅞"

Quarter-Square Triangles

To create this type of triangle, cut a square in half on the diagonal in both directions. A triangle cut in this fashion has the straight of grain on its long side only.

To compute the square needed for this method, determine the finished size of the long side of the triangle. To this figure, add 1¼" and cut a square that size. Now, cut the square in half on both diagonals.

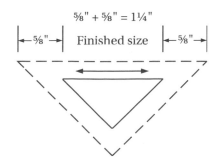

⅝" + ⅝" = 1¼"

⅝"   Finished size   ⅝"

Quarter-square triangles often are used for the set-in corner triangles of a quilt block. In many cases, the long edge is not an easily measured distance, but the short edge is the same size as the block piece next to it.

There are two ways to handle the situation. One is to overestimate the finished size of the long edge of the triangles, set them in, and then cut them to size after the quilt top or block is assembled.

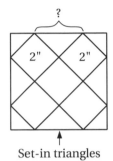

Set-in triangles

The second is to use half-square triangles instead, since these triangles are cut the finished length of the short side. Unfortunately, the bias is also on the long edge of these half-square triangles. Instead, we can cut the squares on point so that the short edges are on the bias and the diagonal of the square is on the straight of grain. When the square is then cut in half, the triangles have the long edge on grain and the short edge is of a specific size.

As an example, let's say we want to produce set-in triangles that are 2" on the short edges but with the grain on the long edge. The necessary squares to cut would measure 2⅞" (2" + ⅞" for half-square triangles) and can be easily cut from the fabric on point using the Bias Square®. Lay the Bias Square on the fabric with its diagonal line on grain and the 2⅞" marks within the boundaries of the fabric. Cut the top two edges, turn the piece around, align the marks with the cut edge, and cut the remaining two sides.

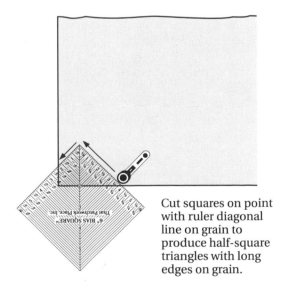

Cut squares on point with ruler diagonal line on grain to produce half-square triangles with long edges on grain.

BARS AND RECTANGLES

Bars and rectangles, such as those used in the Puss in the Corner block here, are cut in the same fashion as squares. A true rectangle is twice as long as it is wide, such as 2" x 4", 3" x 6", for example. Strips are cut ½" wider than the finished width of the shape, and the strips turned sideways. Bars or rectangles (finished length plus ½") are then cut from the strip.

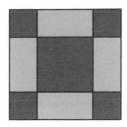

Puss in the Corner

Simple rectangle:

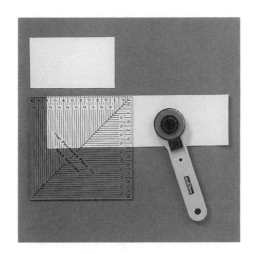

HALF-RECTANGLES

Half-rectangles, like those used in the Star block, are cut from rectangles that are ⅝" larger than the desired finished width and 1¼" longer than the finished length. For instance, if you want two finished half-rectangles, each 2" x 4", cut a full rectangle 2⅝" x 5¼" and then cut it in half on the diagonal. When all seams are sewn, the finished half-rectangle will be the desired finished size.

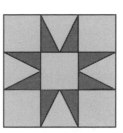

Star

Simple half-rectangle:

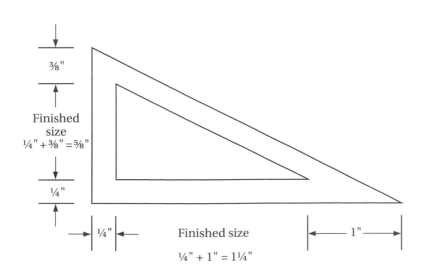

⅜"

Finished
size
¼" + ⅜" = ⅝"

¼"

¼"

Finished size
¼" + 1" = 1¼"

1"

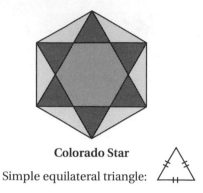

Colorado Star

Simple equilateral triangle:

EQUILATERAL TRIANGLES

Equilateral triangles, such as those used in the Colorado Star block, are triangles that measure the same length on each of the three legs. The angle at each corner is 60°. Cut these triangles from strips of fabric, using the 60° line on your rotary ruler.

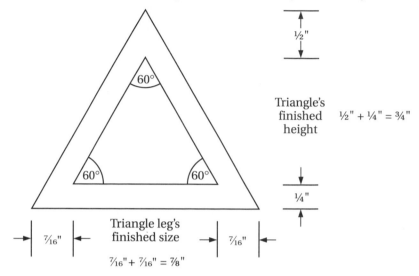

Triangle's finished height   ½" + ¼" = ¾"

Triangle leg's finished size

⁷⁄₁₆" + ⁷⁄₁₆" = ⅞"

Cut straight-of-grain strips that are ¾" wider than the finished height of the triangles. Add ⅞" to the finished length of the triangle leg. On the raw edge of the strip, make marks this distance for as many triangles as you need.

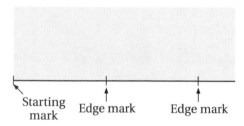

Starting mark   Edge mark   Edge mark

Cut strips ¾" wider than triangle's finished height. Make marks along strip edge ⅞" larger than finished size of triangle leg.

Align the 60° line of the ruler with the raw edge of the strip so that the straight edge of the ruler intersects the first leg mark on the edge. Make a cut from raw edge to raw edge.

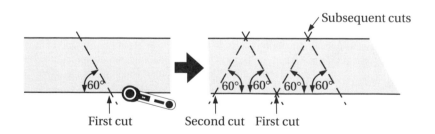

Subsequent cuts

First cut   Second cut   First cut

Rotate your ruler to the opposite side of the strip and continue cutting as many triangles as you need.

DIAMONDS

Full-size diamonds, such as those seen in the LeMoyne Star here, come in three basic, easy-to-cut sizes. These are 30°, 45°, and 60° diamonds. The degree indicates the angle of the narrow points. All three are easy to cut from straight-of-grain strips in the same basic way as for equilateral triangles. Diamonds are squares tilted at an angle. All four sides (legs) measure the same length. In all cases, the strip width is determined by adding ½" to the height of the diamond. To cut diamonds from strips of fabric, measure a certain distance along the edge of the strip (as indicated below) and then cut at an angle to create the diamond. The amount to add to the finished size of the diamond leg, so you know where to mark the strip, varies with each type of diamond.

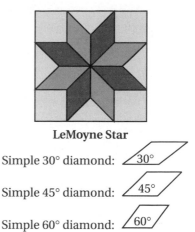

LeMoyne Star

Simple 30° diamond:

Simple 45° diamond:

Simple 60° diamond:

30° diamond: Add 1" to finished leg size. Mark this distance along the raw edge of the strip and cut diamonds by aligning the 30° ruler line with the strip edge.

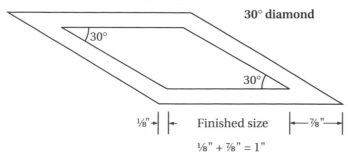

30° diamond

30°

30°

⅛" ← | ← Finished size → | ← ⅞" →

⅛" + ⅞" = 1"

45° diamond: Add ¾" to finished leg size, mark the strip, and cut, using the 45° ruler line.

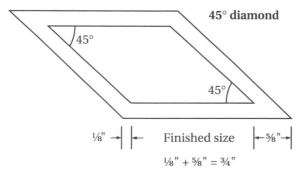

45° diamond

45°

45°

⅛" → | ← Finished size → | ← ⅝" →

⅛" + ⅝" = ¾"

60° diamond: Add ⅝" to finished leg size, mark the strip, and cut, using the 60° ruler line.

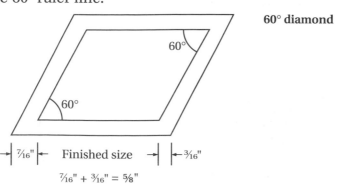

60° diamond

60°

60°

→ | ⁷⁄₁₆" | ← Finished size → | ← ³⁄₁₆"

⁷⁄₁₆" + ³⁄₁₆" = ⅝"

Cutting Guides and the Rotary Cutter

Although one of the basic concepts behind rotary cutting is to avoid the use of templates and hand marking, there are always exceptions. Some shapes, such as triangles with very sharp angles, are too difficult to easily measure for rotary cutting. There are also situations in pattern drafting where $\frac{1}{16}$" rather than $\frac{1}{8}$" increments must be used. Both these situations are best dealt with by combining the use of paper cutting guides with the rotary cutter. There are two basic ways, equally effective, to do this. Cutting guides can also be used to modify one shape into another.

PAPER CUTTING GUIDES

In this method, a cutting guide of the desired shape is cut from tracing paper with seam allowances included. The guide is then taped to the rotary ruler, aligning a straight edge with the edge of the ruler.

If the shape has parallel edges, fabric strips can be cut the width of the guide. Using a cutting guide as a means of measuring strip width is an extremely valuable technique, especially when dealing with widths that are difficult to measure.

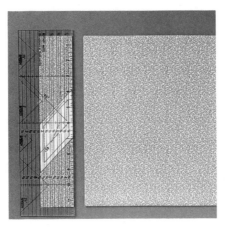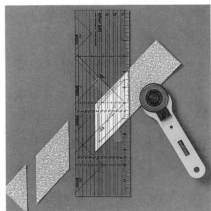

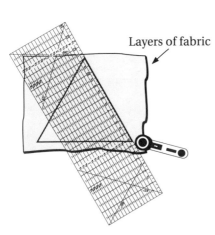

Layers of fabric

Shape is marked on fabric layers and cut all at once with the rotary cutter and ruler.

HARD TEMPLATES

This method is similar to using traditional templates until it comes to cutting. Standard plastic or cardboard templates are prepared with seam allowances included. The shape is marked on one layer of fabric and then cut with the rotary cutter, using the rotary ruler as the cutting guide. The speed of this method can be significantly improved by marking once, then layering four to six pieces of fabric underneath the marking, and cutting through all layers at once.

Be careful of mirror-image shapes. These must be cut from fabric layered with all right sides facing the same direction—right sides up OR right sides down. If an equal number of both images is desired, alternate the fabric directions in the layering.

Mirror-image shapes
are not interchangeable.

MODIFYING SHAPES

Some shapes, such as octagons and trapezoids, are easily made by altering other simple shapes, such as triangles and squares. An octagon, such as the one used in the Snowball block on next page, is created by removing the four corners of a square. A trapezoid, such as the one used in the Castles in the Air block shown here, is a right triangle with its right-angle corner removed; it is created by using a paper template as a cutting guide to modify the parent shape.

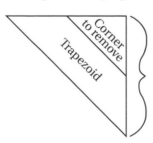

Castles in the Air

Simple trapezoid:

Trapezoids: Draft the trapezoid and parent right triangle. Cut a parent half-square triangle from a fabric square that is ⅞" larger than the finished size of the drafted triangle. See cutting "Half-Square Triangles" on page 13.

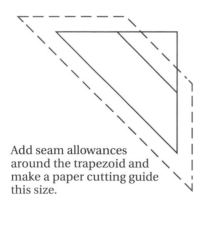

To produce the parent half-square triangle, cut a square this finished size + ⅞". Cut it in half to yield two half-square triangles.

Now, add seam allowances to the drawing of the trapezoid. Make a paper-template guide this size, tape it to the ruler, and use it as a guide to remove the corner of the right triangle.

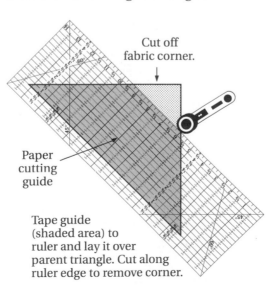

Add seam allowances around the trapezoid and make a paper cutting guide this size.

Cut off fabric corner.

Paper cutting guide

Tape guide (shaded area) to ruler and lay it over parent triangle. Cut along ruler edge to remove corner.

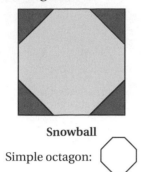

Snowball

Simple octagon:

Octagons: Draft the octagon and parent square. Add seam allowances to the square and cut a fabric square this size.

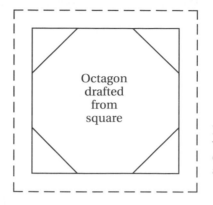

Octagon drafted from square

Parent square is width of finished octagon + seam allowances.

Add seam allowances to the octagon and make a paper cutting guide from it. Tape the guide to the ruler and use it to remove the corners of the parent square, creating an octagon.

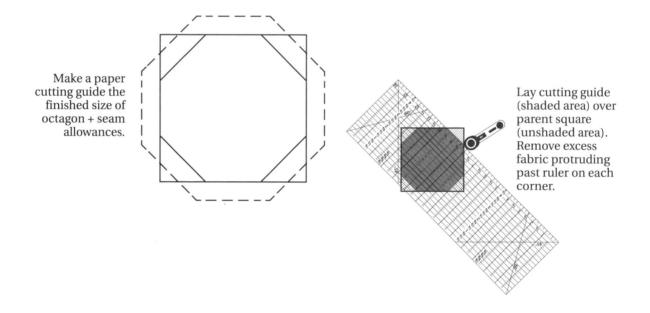

Make a paper cutting guide the finished size of octagon + seam allowances.

Lay cutting guide (shaded area) over parent square (unshaded area). Remove excess fabric protruding past ruler on each corner.

DESIGN CONSIDERATIONS

Another way to use hard templates in conjunction with rotary cutting is for design considerations. There are times when you may wish to position a particular part of a fabric design on one or more of the pattern pieces. The best way to accomplish this is with the use of see-through plastic templates so that each piece can be manually marked and cut from the desired area. Templates are constructed with seam allowances included and marked on the fabric before cutting with the rotary cutter.

Take a look at the LeMoyne Star table pad on page 27. Each diamond was cut from the exact same repeat of the border design so that, after piecing was completed, the print created a secondary design.

Nubbing Points for Sewing

Nubbing points removes excess fabric that extends past the seam allowances. In this way, fabric pieces are easily matched when preparing to sew.

Shapes with 90° and 45° angles are easily nubbed at the ¼" seam lines, as illustrated at right, on quarter-square and half-square triangles.

For many situations, I find it easiest to make paper templates with seam allowances included and sewing lines drawn. Then I lay the paper pieces together as if they are to be sewn, match sewing lines, and trim the excess paper beyond the seam allowances. These trimmed paper pieces become my guides for nubbing the points on my fabric pieces.

Some shapes, such as half-square and quarter-square triangles, are easily nubbed without templates—using simple addition.

Align sewing lines of paper cutting guides and remove excess points. Use to nub all corresponding fabric pieces for easy matching when sewing.

HALF-SQUARE TRIANGLES

Add ½" to the finished dimension of the triangle's short side. (If this measurement is an odd size, use the paper-template method described above to determine where to nub the points.) Lay the Bias Square® along the raw edges of the triangle and cut off the excess points extending beyond both side edges.

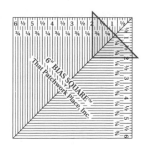

QUARTER-SQUARE TRIANGLES

Two measurements are needed to nub these triangles since they are being nubbed perpendicular to the long edge. Both measurements are based on the finished size of this long edge. (If the long edge is an odd size, use the paper-template method described on page 21.) If you can measure the long edge, add ⅞" to the finished size and measure this distance from the left corner toward the right and remove the excess fabric to the right of the cutting guide.

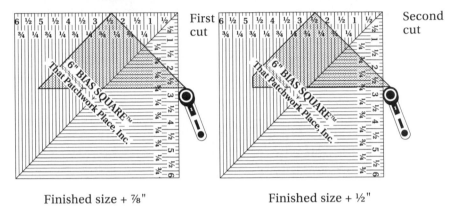

Finished size + ⅞"   Finished size + ½"

Now, add ½" to the finished size, turn the triangle over, and measure from the one nubbed edge to the right, again removing excess fabric to the right of the cutting guide.

Straight-of-Grain Strip Piecing

Until now, we've discussed the use of the rotary cutter to quickly cut simple shapes that are then matched and sewn. The only real variation on traditional techniques has been in how the shapes were cut. Fortunately, rotary cutting can take us beyond fast cutting into the world of quick piecing by combining cutting techniques with the sewing machine. These techniques involve using both straight-of-grain and bias strip piecing, and the myriad of manipulations that can occur as a result.

BASIC CONCEPT

Cutting squares and sewing them together is the traditional way to assemble the simple Ninepatch block. Whether the cutting is done with scissors or a rotary cutter, the basic construction process is the same. Many complex patterns can only be assembled in this simple, straightforward fashion, but a multitude of designs, including the humble Ninepatch, can be quickly assembled in large quantities using innovative construction processes.

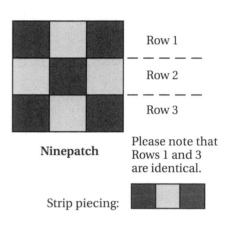

Ninepatch

Row 1

Row 2

Row 3

Please note that Rows 1 and 3 are identical.

Strip piecing:

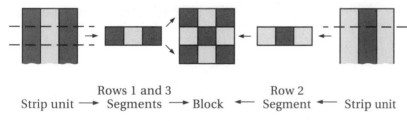

Strip unit → Segments → Block ← Segment ← Strip unit

Rows 1 and 3 Segments — Row 2 Segment

If we break the Ninepatch block into rows, we can see that there are two types of rows. Rather than cut individual squares, we can cut strips, sew the strips side by side, then cut segments (presewn rows) from this newly formed strip unit. Sew two types of strip units—one for each type of row—and speed the piecing process by doing all the "block" sewing at one time without stopping and matching before each seam. Since the resulting squares should be on the straight of grain, the strips are cut on grain, perpendicular to the fold of the fabric.

CUTTING STRIPS AND ASSEMBLING STRIP UNITS

Begin by preparing your fabric for cutting as outlined in "Getting Ready," page 10. Since we want the resulting squares to be cut on grain, the strips need to be cut on grain also. Follow the instructions for cutting "Strips," page 12.

Strips are cut the desired finished width of the square plus ½" to account for the seam allowance on either side of the strip. The length of strip to cut is determined by multiplying the number of segments to be cut by the width of each segment with seam allowances included. It's a good idea to add a few inches to this length to account for human error.

Assemble the strip unit by sewing the strips together, side by side, using the proper ¼" seam allowance. Generally, seams are pressed toward the darker fabric unless there is a reason to press them in a different direction.

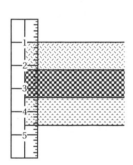

To cut segments, turn the strip unit sideways so that one short end can be "trued up." Lay a horizontal ruler line on one of the seam lines near the short edge of the strip unit. If the seams are straight, they should align with or be parallel to a ruler line. Keeping everything in line, move the ruler up to the edge of the strip unit and cut off any unevenness at the edge. Even if the edges are straight, it's a good idea to trim the ends to give a clean cut and eliminate any rough starts on the seams. This true edge is the guide you need to make segment cuts at right angles to the seam.

Once the strip unit is trimmed, cut segments according to your pattern needs. Begin with the freshly cut end of the strip unit and measure in the prescribed distance for the segment. Never make a segment cut without also placing a horizontal ruler line along one of the interior seams. It is very important that the cut be at right angles to the seams. Ideally, the upper and lower raw edges should also align, but, if necessary, you can make adjustments to these when the final seams are sewn. An interior seam is already locked in and will appear slanted if the cut is not made at right angles to it.

If, at any time, the short edge and interior seams no longer form a right angle, the edge needs to be trued up again. This happens periodically and shouldn't cause concern. It is due to the minuscule amount of ruler slippage that occurs with each cut. Of course, the more carefully you cut, the less frequently you will have to recut the edges.

The cut segments can then be sewn together to form a Ninepatch block. If the various strip-unit seams are always pressed toward the darker fabric, the seams where the rows meet end up facing opposite directions. These are called opposing seam allowances and are highly desirable since they butt next to each other and form a tight intersection that is easily and accurately sewn. Pressing seams so they butt at intersections is important to keep in mind when planning the pressing pattern for your patchwork blocks.

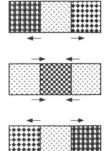

When seams that meet at an intersection are pressed in opposite directions, they butt tightly when aligned for sewing.

As you look at quilt designs in books and patterns, you will find many opportunities to use strip piecing in place of traditional piecing.

Gallery of Quilts

Woodland Tree by Donna Thomas, 1990, Dorf-Guell, Germany, 36" x 36". Strip piecing and layered cutting of the tree triangles resulted in a five-hour quilt top.

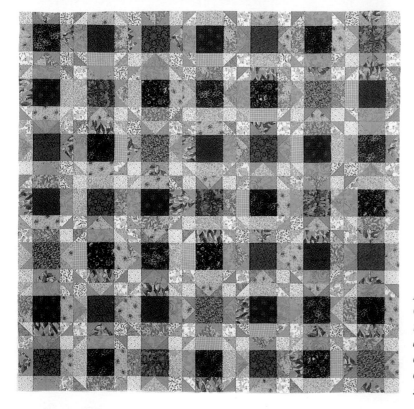

First Star by Donna Thomas, 1989, Frankfurt, Germany, 70" x 70". As quick as this piece was to make, yet another household move was quicker, preventing the project's intended completion as a shower curtain. It is constructed from bias squares, simple squares, and rectangles.

Snowball by Nancy J. Martin, 1985, Woodinville, Washington, 40" x 58". The striking overall pattern is created by modifying squares into octagons to create Snowball blocks that are then alternated with scrappy, strip-pieced Ninepatch blocks. Quilted by Andrea Scadden. (Collection of That Patchwork Place, Inc., Bothell, Washington)

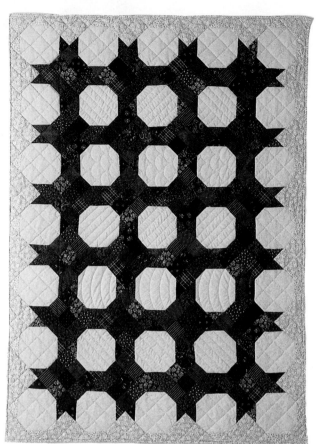

Waterwheel by Donna Thomas, 1987, Brookhaven, Pennsylvania, 26" x 26". Almost a charm quilt—can you find the three fabric repeats?—this inviting wall quilt is quick to make, using side-striped, half-square triangles.

Goose in the Pond by Donna Thomas, 1989, Frankfurt, Germany, 60" x 75½". A traditional color combination and an intricate-looking design disguise a simple construction process. Bias squares and straight-of-grain strip piecing make this an easily assembled quilt to grace a young boy's bed.

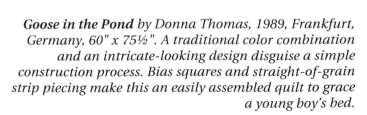

Burgoyne Surrounded *by Nancy J. Martin, 1989, Woodinville, Washington, 69" x 85". An intricate pattern becomes a breeze when strip-piecing techniques are used. (Collection of That Patchwork Place, Inc., Bothell, Washington)*

LeMoyne Star table pad *by Donna Thomas, 1988, Brookhaven, Pennsylvania, 15" x 15". The use of a repeat pattern in the plain diamonds creates an exciting, overall secondary design. Each diamond was individually marked and cut with the rotary cutter to exactly repeat the design.*

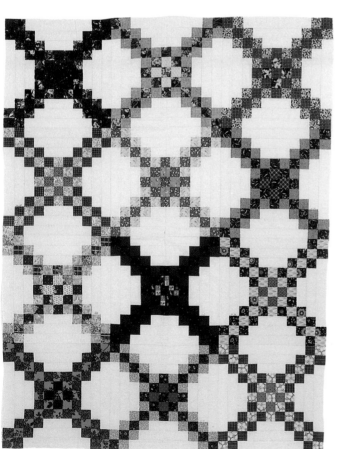

Friendship Quilt *by Donna Thomas, Joan Scone, and Kathy Meredith, 1988, Swarthmore, Pennsylvania, Chadds Ford, Pennsylvania, and Frankfurt, Germany, 54" x 76". This friendship quilt was inspired by an antique quilt seen in Sara Nephew's book* My Mother's Quilts: Designs from the Thirties. *A medley of fabrics and strip-piecing techniques increased the joy of sharing with friends. (Collection of author)*

***Star of the East** quilt block by Donna Thomas, 1991, Dorf-Guell, Germany, 10¼" x 10¼". This light and airy springtime block required only half the usual assembly time; the secret—strip-pieced half-diamonds.*

***Crazy Ann quilt block** by Donna Thomas, 1987, Brookhaven, Pennsylvania, 12" x 12". Someday, this pretty little block will be part of a sampler quilt but, for now, it is an excellent example of how to use strip-pieced rectangles.*

***Broken Star**, maker unknown, 1932, South Dakota, 76" x 78". The beautiful pastel, pieced diamonds in this quilt were undoubtedly labored over for many hours to result in such a breathtaking quilt. Quick cutting and piecing would cut the time to a minimum today. (Collection of Nancy J. Martin, Woodinville, Washington)*

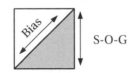

Bias Strip Piecing

BASIC CONCEPT

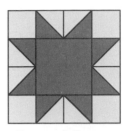

Sawtooth Star

Bias square:

The most common use of bias strip piecing is to quick-cut pieced bias squares. A bias square is a square composed of two right triangles joined together on the long side. This particular type of triangle combination is used extensively in both traditional and contemporary quilt patterns. The Sawtooth Star shown here is one such design. In most situations, the outside edges of a bias square should be cut on the straight of grain to avoid stretching. This means that the seam running across the diagonal of the square is on the bias.

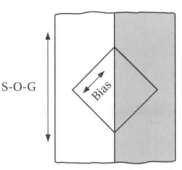

Strips are cut on straight of grain. Cut squares have edges on bias.

If two fabric strips of appropriate width are sewn together as in "Straight-of-Grain Strip Piecing" (pages 23–24), squares may be cut from these strips on point to yield presewn bias squares.

If the strips are cut on grain as in straight-of-grain strip piecing, then the resulting squares have the bias on the four outer edges and the straight of grain on the diagonal seam, which is not what we want. If we cut the strips on the bias, the resulting squares then have outer edges on the straight of grain.

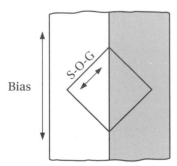

Strips are cut on bias grain. Cut squares have edges on straight of grain.

This basic idea is the key to the bias-square system. Bias strips are cut and sewn together. Bias squares are then cut diagonally from the bias strip unit. There are several things you need to know, though, before proceeding. For instance:

1. How do you cut bias strips?
2. What size strips do you cut?
3. How do you cut squares from the bias strip units?

The following sections will help answer these and other questions you may have.

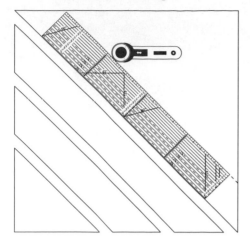

CUTTING BIAS STRIPS

If the diagonal of any square cut on the straight of grain is on the bias, then strips cut from the diagonal of a square will have bias edges. Begin by making a center diagonal cut through a fabric square. Using the long center edge as the cutting guide, you can then cut strips from each large triangle.

In fact, a complete square is unnecessary as long as the two edges of one corner are cut at a right angle. Measure an equal distance (x) along each right-angle side and make a mark. Make the first diagonal cut from point to point and proceed as with a regular square.

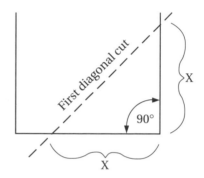

To save time, cut the bias strips for the two fabrics that will be sewn together for the bias squares at the same time. Steam press them *right sides facing up* (so they adhere slightly when steamed), cut the square or right-angle sides, and begin cutting the diagonal strips. Half-yard pieces are a good size to use, because you can cut sufficiently long strips.

ASSEMBLING BIAS STRIP UNITS

Bias strips are sewn with a ¼" seam along their longest edges. Press seams toward the darker fabric unless there is a specific need for them to be pressed in a different direction. They may be sewn in simple pairs or with several strips across to form a multiple bias strip unit.

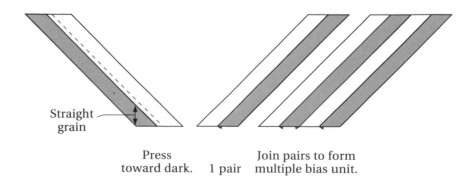

Straight grain

Press toward dark.   1 pair   Join pairs to form multiple bias unit.

DETERMINING STRIP WIDTH

The width you cut bias strips depends on whether you are sewing simple pairs or multiple bias strip units. When only sewing two bias strips together, cut the strips the width of the unfinished bias square. For instance, if you are cutting a 3" unfinished bias square (2½" finished), then cut the bias strips 3" wide.

When sewing multiple bias strips, cut the bias strips ¼" wider than the unfinished bias square to account for the extra seam. For instance, to cut a 3" unfinished bias square from a multiple bias strip unit, cut bias strips 3¼" wide.

With some of the larger bias squares, I have found that the strips are sometimes much wider (never smaller!) than really needed, using the above method. Normally, this is not a concern, but if you have a limited amount of fabric, it is desirable to know more precisely how wide the strips need to be. In this case, draw the bias-square triangle with seam allowances included and measure the distance from the outer corner to the diagonal. Round this figure up to the nearest ⅛" and cut bias strips this size. If you plan to sew multiple bias strip units, cut the bias strips ¼" wider than this to account for the extra seam.

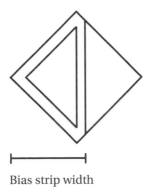

Bias strip width

CUTTING BIAS SQUARES

Once the bias strips are cut and sewn together, bias squares may be cut from the bias strip unit, using the Bias Square®. The ⅛" markings on two sides mean that you can easily cut a large variety of bias squares. For odd-sized bias squares, tape a paper cutting guide (page 18) to the corner of the Bias Square. A diagonal line bisecting the ruler makes it easy to establish your cutting line.

Begin with the lower end of the bias strip unit and place the Bias Square over the lower edge of the strips, with the diagonal line on top of the seam. The dimension of the template or desired markings on the ruler should be just inside the lower raw edges of the strip. Cut the two top edges of the square from raw edge to raw edge. Set the resulting piece aside and continue to cut as many bias squares from the strip unit as possible, being sure that the markings are always within the strip-unit boundaries and not extending past the lower point.

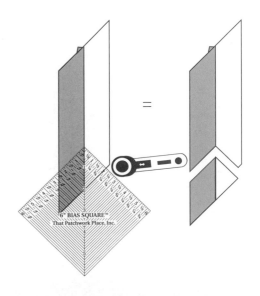

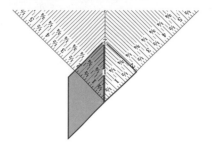

Go back to each bias square and turn it 180°, with the lower two edges up; then, trim edges to size with the Bias Square®.

When cutting bias squares from multiple bias strip units, use the same procedure, being careful to always cut from the lowest points across the bias strip unit before cutting farther up the strip unit. Move systematically from either left to right or right to left, cutting all the low points first.

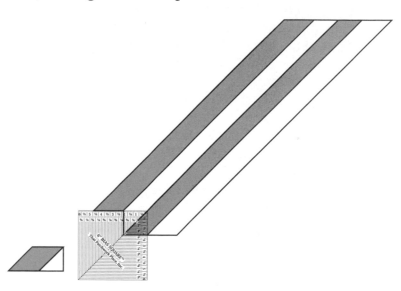

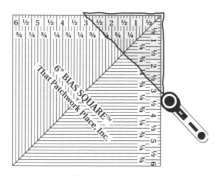

Square off the corner of edge triangle.

As you cut bias squares from bias strip units, you will notice that there are edge triangles left over along the outer edges of the strips. You will also notice that fewer edge triangles are produced when you cut from multiple bias strip units than from simple bias strip units. If large enough, these edge triangles can be used in many patterns that require singly cut triangles.

Before using edge triangles, they must be sized. The diagonal edge may also need adjustment.

Use the corner of your Bias Square to check and square off the corner of the triangle. Then, nub the triangle points. Next, align the 45° line on your Bias Square with one of the short sides of the triangle, and adjust the ¼" line so that it runs from inside point to inside point on the nubbed long edge of the triangle. Trim away all excess past the edge.

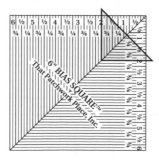

Nub the triangle points.

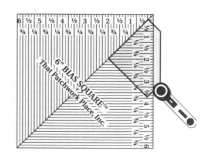

Trim excess.

Creating Scrap Quilts

Scrap quilts can be created using strip-piecing techniques. Cut strips from a wide variety of fabrics, substituting dark and light fabrics for the same positions instead of one or two specific prints. Seam the strips together and cut the desired segments or bias squares from them. For example, to create a scrappy Ninepatch, choose a variety of dark and light prints. Cut straight-of-grain strips and seam them alternately, dark-light-dark and light-dark-light, to create the two types of strip units needed. I used this technique to make the scrappy Puss in the Corner blocks found in the Woodland Tree quilt top shown on page 25.

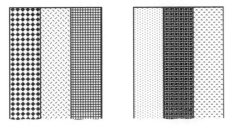

Scrappy straight-of-grain strip units

Bias strip units can be assembled in the same fashion to create scrappy bias squares. Sew a wide variety of light and dark bias strips together and cut bias squares from this multiple bias strip unit. An example that includes this technique is the First Star quilt on page 25.

Scrappy bias strip units

You can use the ScrapSaver™, a rotary cutting guide designed by Judy Hopkins, to quickly resize the edge triangles that result from cutting bias squares. Judy created it to make it easy to quick-cut half-square triangles from your scraps without tedious calculations or the need for templates.

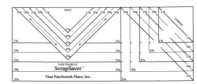

ScrapSaver™

Other Uses of Strip Piecing

The basic concepts of both straight-of-grain and bias strip piecing can be applied in a number of ways to create shortcuts for many presewn shapes. Following are some examples.

SIDE-BY-SIDES

Side-by-side triangles consist of two quarter-square triangles that are joined to each other on one of their short legs rather than along the diagonal. Side-by-side triangles can be seen in the Ohio Star block.

Note that in a block such as the Ohio Star, the long edges of the four triangles making up the square should be on the straight of grain as indicated by the arrows in the diagram.

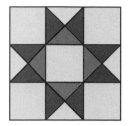

Ohio Star

Side-by-Side:

 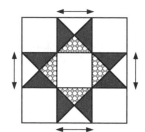

Each side-by-side is made up of two quarter-square triangles.

Long edges of the four triangles should be on the straight of grain.

The quick method for constructing side-by-sides is a variation on bias-square construction. If you cut a bias square in half on the diagonal, you end up with two sets of side-by-side triangles. Each set is the mirror image of its mate.

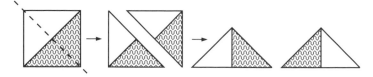

Before you start cutting, you need to know:

1. The desired finished size of the long edge of the side-by-side units;
2. The size of the bias square you will need to cut to yield the correct size of the side-by-side unit;
3. The width of the bias strip you will need to cut to make the bias strip unit.

Draft the pattern on graph paper and measure the long edge of the quarter-square triangle composing the side-by-side unit.

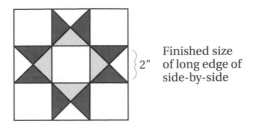

Finished size of long edge of side-by-side

Measure long edge of side-by-side. Add ⅞" to determine size of bias square. In this example, a 2⅞" (2" + ⅞") bias square is needed.

Think of the side-by-side unit as if it is a half-square triangle that you will be cutting from a square. If you are making half-square triangles (page 13), you may remember that the magic number to add to the finished size of the triangle is ⅞". The same number applies to cutting bias squares large enough to produce side-by-sides. Add ⅞" to the desired finished size of the long edge of the quarter-square triangle and cut bias squares that size from the bias strip unit.

Cut bias strips for this size bias square, following the same procedures as outlined in "Cutting Bias Strips" on page 30. Assemble the bias strip unit and cut bias squares from it as described in "Cutting Bias Squares" on pages 31–32.

Example: If you want to produce presewn, side-by-side units that will be 2" finished size on the long edge, cut 2⅞" bias squares (2" + ⅞" = 2⅞"). The size of the bias strips needed to form a multiple bias strip unit is ¼" larger than the bias square (2⅞" + ¼" = 3⅛").

Once the 2⅞" bias squares are cut, cut them in half on the unseamed diagonal.

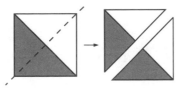

If you ever need the long edges of the quarter-square triangles in the side-by-sides on the bias, cut straight-of-grain strips instead of bias strips. The rest of the process remains the same.

STRIPED SQUARES

King's Cross

Simple
striped square:

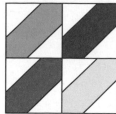

Indian Hatchet

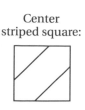

Center
striped square:

Land of the Midnight Sun

Offset
striped square:

Roman Stripe

Multiple offset
striped square:

Striped squares have stripes running through the diagonal of the block. These units are used frequently in many quilt patterns, such as the ones shown here. They can have three or more stripes running through the block or can be offset to one side as in Roman Stripe. The rules for assembly are the same for each of the striped squares shown here, whether there is one stripe or many.

Striped squares are cut from strip units just like bias squares. Depending on where you wish to place the straight of grain in the finished unit, strips are cut either on grain or on the bias. You will find in most instances that bias strips are required. The strip width is determined by the desired finished width of the stripes. It is best if the center stripes are an easily measured size, but the outer stripes forming the corners can be odd widths that are rounded up to the nearest ⅛".

Begin by drafting the block with measurable center stripes. Add ½" to the finished width of each center stripe and cut strips this width. Measure the corner stripes from the inner seam to the corner point, rounding up to the nearest ⅛", and add ⅝" to this figure. Cut strips this size for the outer strips. Assemble the strip unit as you would normally.

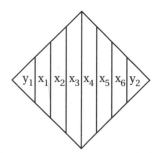

Number and width of center stripes can vary. (Here they are x_1-x_6.) They are cut ½" wider than desired finished width. Outer strips (y_1, y_2) are rounded up to nearest ⅛" and cut ⅝" larger than this figure.

The squares you cut from this strip unit will be ½" larger than the desired finished size, just as with any simple square. If your block has a stripe centered over the diagonal of the square as in the Simple Striped Square, you will need to have a diagonal guide for centering your cutting guide on the strip unit. Create one by either pressing or drawing a line through the middle of the center strip with a wash-out chalk pencil or wheel. Now align the diagonal line on your cutting guide or Bias Square® with the line on your strip unit and cut squares, following the instructions for "Cutting Bias Squares" on pages 31–32.

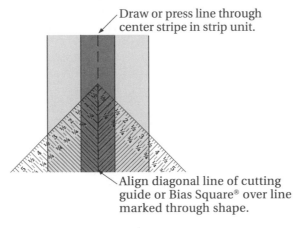

Draw or press line through center stripe in strip unit.

Align diagonal line of cutting guide or Bias Square® over line marked through shape.

Multiple strip units can also be constructed by reversing the order of the strips in the strip unit and sewing many strips together. Be sure to add another ¼" to the width of the outer strips in the simple strip unit before building multiple strip units to account for the extra seam where the reverse begins.

Many blocks can be created by repeating strip-unit order in reverse direction.

Repeat seam.
Cut strips at this seam an additional ¼" wider to accommodate extra seam allowance.

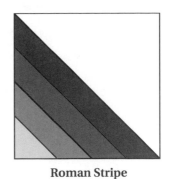

Roman Stripe

2" cut size
1½" finished size

STRIPED HALF-SQUARE TRIANGLES

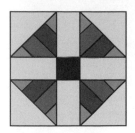

All Dressed Up

Basic-striped
half-square
triangle:

Dutch Windmill

Offset-striped
half-square
triangle:

Sparkler

Center-striped
half-square
triangle:

If you cut striped squares in half perpendicular to the seams, you produce two half-square triangles.

Strip units are assembled exactly as you would for striped squares except that the outer strips are cut ⅞" wider than the finished width. The squares cut from the strip unit need to be ⅞" larger than the finished short edge of the triangle. The two triangles from each square are mirror images of each other and, thus, not always interchangeable.

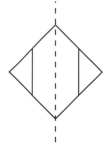

Center-striped square cut in
half through center stripe

Center-Striped, Half-Square Triangles: The strip-unit assembly is slightly different when you decide to cut a center-striped square in half through the center stripe instead of perpendicular to the stripes. This cut produces stripes parallel to the long edge of the triangle.

When planning the strip unit for this type of triangle, cut the center stripe 1" wider than desired finished size to accommodate the two seams that will eventually be sewn on either side of the cut. If you wish to produce a triangle like the one in Castles in the Air, first measure the finished width of the two stripes. As an example, let's say the large stripe measures 1" wide when finished. The corner stripe measures 1⅛" when finished.

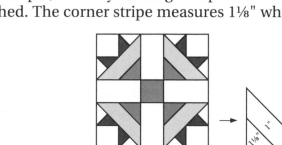

Castles in the Air

Since the center strip in the square will be cut in half to create a 1" stripe in each of the two triangles, it needs to be cut twice as wide (2") plus extra for seam allowances. To this figure, add ½" for the seam on either side of the strip in the strip unit and another ½" for the seams that will be sewn later on either side of the cut, through the center of the strip unit. The total to add to the doubled finished size then is 1" (2" + 1" = 3"-wide strip). The corner stripes are cut ⅝" wider than the finished size, as usual.

Assemble the strip unit and cut the squares as you would for any striped triangle. Then, cut the squares in half through the center stripe.

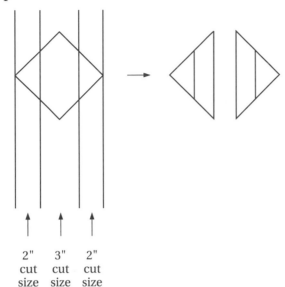

2"
cut
size

3"
cut
size

2"
cut
size

Side-Striped, Half-Square Triangles: The last type of pieced triangle has stripes running parallel to one of the short sides of the triangle.

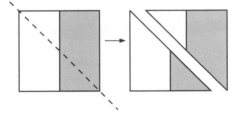

S-O-G

Side-striped
half-square
triangle:

Waterwheel

It can be easily cut from another type of striped square. Be aware that the two triangles produced are opposites in color placement just as in side-by-sides.

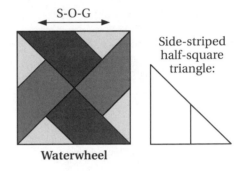

Again, strips are cut to form the strip unit, and squares are cut from the strip unit. These squares are then cut in half on the diagonal to produce triangles.

The strips that will go on the outer edges of the strip unit are cut ⅞" wider than the desired finished size to accommodate the seam allowance and corner. If there is only a total of two strips, they are both cut ⅞" wider. Any center strips are cut ½" wider than the desired finished size.

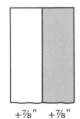

+⅞" +⅞"

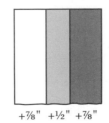

+⅞" +½" +⅞"

Cut outer strips ⅞"
wider than desired
finished size.

With a two-strip
unit, cut both strips
⅞" wider.

In strip units with more than
two strips, outer strips are ⅞"
wider than finished size,
while inner strip(s) are ½"
wider than finished size.

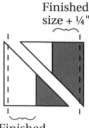

Cut a square from the strip unit that is 1¼" larger than the triangle's short leg.

Short leg
+
1¼"

Finished size + ¼"

Trim outer strips in each triangle to finished size + ¼" from seam.

Finished size + ¼"

Squares are cut 1¼" wider than the finished size of the short edge of the triangle and then cut in half to yield two triangles.

One additional step is required to trim the triangles to the desired size. To be able to use both triangles, the short leg of the triangle opposite the corner triangle must be trimmed to the finished size, plus ¼".

At first glance, you might wonder why the triangle was not cut narrower to begin with. On closer examination, you will realize that if this had been done, the second triangle created would not have a corner triangle the desired size. The ⅞" is added to accommodate the triangles produced at each side of the square when it is cut. If you do not plan on using both triangles, it is only necessary to cut the one outer strip of the unneeded section ½" wider than the finished size.

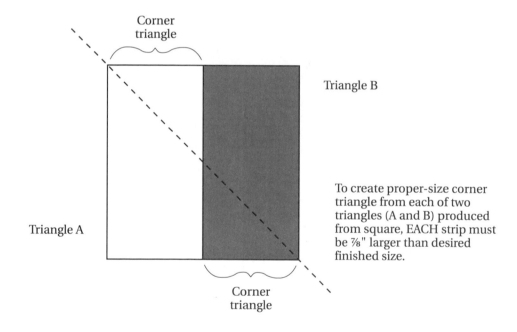

Corner triangle

Triangle B

Triangle A

Corner triangle

To create proper-size corner triangle from each of two triangles (A and B) produced from square, EACH strip must be ⅞" larger than desired finished size.

STRIP-PIECED RECTANGLES

Generally, a rectangle is an elongated square that is twice as long as it is wide, for example, 1" x 2", 2" x 4", or 3" x 6". Just as with squares, the sides should be on the straight of grain. This means that the diagonal seam is on the bias, although, in the case of a rectangle, it is not a true 45° bias. In the text that follows, this bias angle is called "off bias."

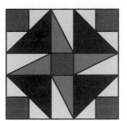

Crazy Ann

Pieced rectangle:

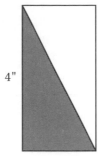

2"
Pieced rectangle

Pieced rectangles are assembled from two elongated triangles and can be strip pieced in a fashion similar to bias squares. Mary Hickey has developed a wonderful system for strip piecing these bias-rectangles, using the BiRangle™ cutting guide, in her book *Angle Antics*.

To cut strips for pieced rectangles, begin by preparing the fabric edges for cutting as outlined on page 11. Arrange one layer of each of the two fabrics comprising the rectangle together, *right sides up*, with the selvages to the left and right as in the diagram. Half-yard pieces are a good size to use, because you can cut sufficiently long strips.

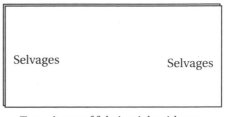

Two pieces of fabric, right sides up

If mirror-image versions of the pieced rectangle are desired, the fabric may be layered by folding it so all four selvages are together. By layering this way, you will be cutting an equal number of mirror-image strips, that is, an equal number face up and face down.

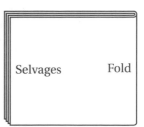

Two pieces of fabric, right sides up, and then folded in half, selvage to selvage

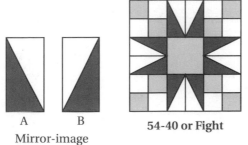

A   B
Mirror-image
strip-pieced rectangles

54-40 or Fight

- To cut strip-pieced rectangles like Unit A, cut strips with both fabrics face up.
- To cut strip-pieced rectangles like Unit B, cut strips with both fabrics face down.
- To cut both types at once, position both fabrics face up and then fold in half selvages to selvages.

Make an oversized half-rectangle template, about 4" x 8". Use a hard template material, such as cardboard or plastic. Align the right-angle corner of the template with the lower-left corner of the prepared fabric. Lay your rotary ruler next to the diagonal edge of the template and move them together to the right, keeping the template even with the cut edge until the ruler intersects the upper-left corner of the fabric. If you are using a ½-yard piece of fabric, you will probably need a 24"-long ruler. Keeping the ruler in place, remove the template guide and cut away the corner of fabric to the left of the ruler. Use this diagonal cut as the starting point for cutting strips. By using the diagonal of the rectangle as the bias guide, you should produce strips at the correct angle to yield rectangles on grain.

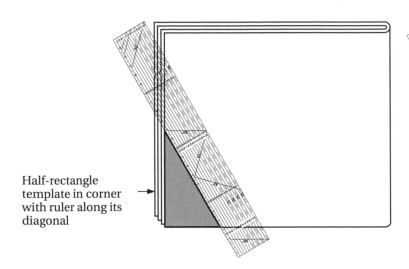

Half-rectangle template in corner with ruler along its diagonal

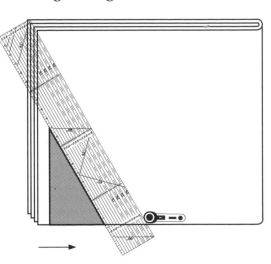

Move template and ruler together to right until ruler intersects upper-left corner of fabric. Cut along edge of ruler.

The width of the strips to be cut will be based on the desired finished size of the pieced rectangle and whether you are sewing simple pairs or multiple strips. For simple pairs of strips, add ½" and cut off-bias strips this width. (This allows for ¼" seam allowances and requires careful, accurate stitching so points of the triangles meet exactly at the corners of the rectangles.) For instance, if you want a pieced rectangle of 2", cut off-bias strips 2½" wide.

STRIP WIDTHS FOR MULTIPLE STRIP UNITS		
Finished Rectangle		Cut Width of Diagonal Strip
Short side	Long side	
¾"	1½"	1¾"
1"	2"	2"
1¼"	2½"	2¼"
1½"	3"	2½"
1¾"	3½"	2¾"
2"	4"	3"
2¼"	4½"	3¼"
2½"	5"	3½"
2¾"	5½"	3¾"
3"	6"	4"
3¼"	6½"	4¼"
3½"	7"	4½"

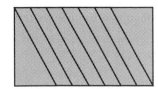 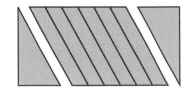

If you are sewing multiple pairs of strips together, use the chart to determine the strip width needed.

If you layered the fabric to produce two types of rectangles, separate the strips into piles according to whether they were face up or face down in the fabric layers. Sew the strips from each pile into pairs or multiple strip units.

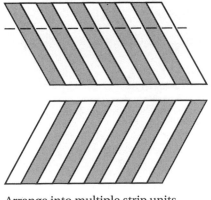

Arrange into multiple strip units

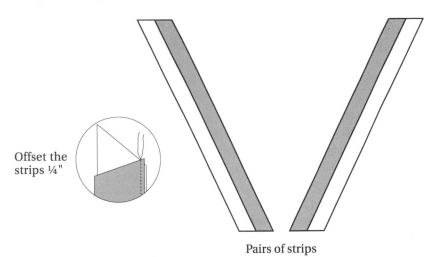

Offset the strips ¼"

Pairs of strips

To cut bias rectangles from simple pairs of strips, use the BiRangle™ ruler, designed by Mary Hickey to accompany her bias-rectangle technique. Align the diagonal line of either the BiRangle™ ruler with the seam of the strips, as in the diagram. Beginning at the top of the strips, cut the first two sides of the rectangle.

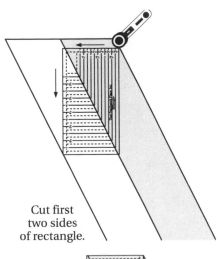

Cut first two sides of rectangle.

Turn the BiRangle or cutting guide, realign the diagonal line, and cut the remaining two sides of the rectangle. Continue to cut as many pieced rectangles as you need.

To cut rectangles from the pieced strips slanting to the right, I find it easiest to turn the strips over, face down, and cut from the wrong side of the fabric. These strips yield rectangles that are mirror images of the strips slanted to the left. Keep this in mind when planning your fabric-strip color arrangements.

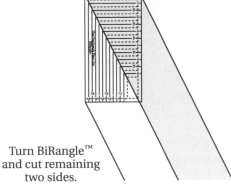

Turn BiRangle™ and cut remaining two sides.

Multiple sewn strips are cut in the same manner, cutting the first two sides across the row of strips. These segments are then turned so the remaining two sides of the rectangle can be cut.

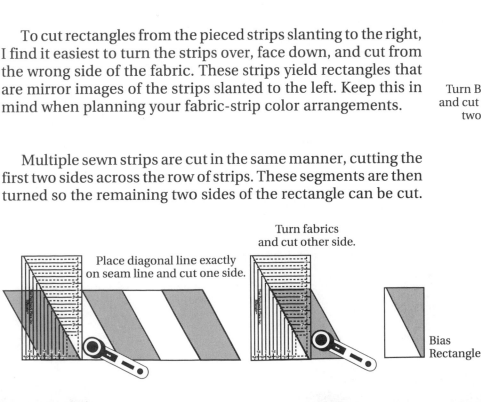

Turn fabrics and cut other side.

Place diagonal line exactly on seam line and cut one side.

Bias Rectangle

Star of the East

Half-length pieced diamond:

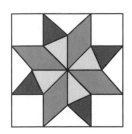

King's Star

Half-width pieced diamond:

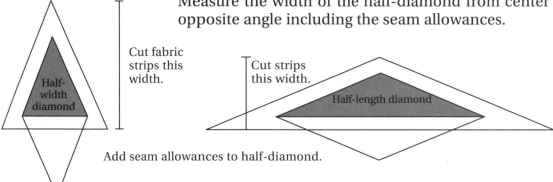

Cut fabric strips this width.

Half-width diamond

Add seam allowances to half-diamond.

STRIP-PIECED DIAMONDS

Any type of diamond can be strip-pieced, although the most commonly used diamonds in quiltmaking are 30°, 45°, or 60° diamonds. Remember that true diamonds have four legs that all measure the same length. The slenderest of these diamonds is the 30° diamond. It has a 30° angle at its narrow points and requires twelve diamonds to complete a circle. A 45° diamond will need eight per circle, and the 60° diamond, only six around a circle.

Simple Strip-Pieced Half-Diamonds: All three of these diamonds can be easily presewn in halves, either across the width or length, using basic strip-piecing methods.

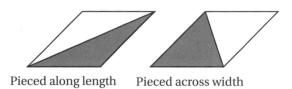

Pieced along length   Pieced across width

As always, begin by drafting the half-diamond needed. Add seam allowances and make a paper cutting guide this size. Measure the width of the half-diamond from center seam to opposite angle including the seam allowances.

Cut strips this width.

Half-length diamond

Cut straight-of-grain fabric strips this width and seam them, right sides together, on *both* raw edges. Tape the paper guide to your rotary ruler with one of the exterior legs of the diamond aligned with the edge of the ruler. Align the center the diamond with the raw edge of the fabric strips and make a cut.

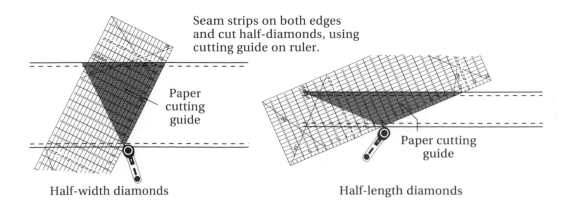

Seam strips on both edges and cut half-diamonds, using cutting guide on ruler.

Paper cutting guide

Paper cutting guide

Half-width diamonds   Half-length diamonds

Turn the cut piece over and align the cutting guide over the first cut edge. Trim up the second side. Continue in this way, cutting as many diamonds as you need. Remove the few stitches at the points and press the diamonds open.

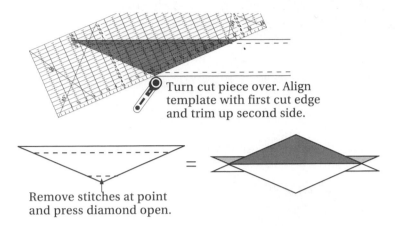

Turn cut piece over. Align template with first cut edge and trim up second side.

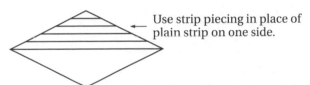

Remove stitches at point and press diamond open.

String-Pieced Half-Diamonds: Using the same principles as above, substitute one multipieced strip for a plain strip in the strip unit. It could be strip-pieced parallel or perpendicular to the seam. Diamonds cut from this stripping would then be solid on one-half and string-pieced on the other half.

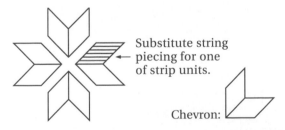

Use strip piecing in place of plain strip on one side.

Fiesta!

String-pieced diamond:

Chevrons: Create pieced full diamonds (chevrons) by cutting simple, full-sized diamonds as described on page 17, using pairs of strips sewn together on one raw edge. Pairs of chevrons can be joined to form a star.

Substitute string piecing for one of strip units.

Chevron:

Draft the single diamond. Cut strips the width of the diamond, plus seam allowances. Seam strips into pairs along one edge but do not press. Following the instructions for simple, cut diamonds, measure and cut the desired-size diamond (30°, 45°, or 60°) from the strip unit, using either the ruler angle markings or a paper cutting guide. Again, for a more elaborate chevron or diamond pair, string-piece one of the strips in the strip unit.

Virginia Star

Diamonds within diamonds: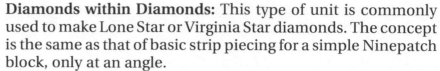

Diamonds within Diamonds: This type of unit is commonly used to make Lone Star or Virginia Star diamonds. The concept is the same as that of basic strip piecing for a simple Ninepatch block, only at an angle.

Draft the diamond. Think of it as a square on a slant. Divide it into an equal number of segments across and down; for example, three across and three down or four across and four down. Draw the inner lines parallel to the outer diamond legs. Decide on the fabrics for each segment and color.

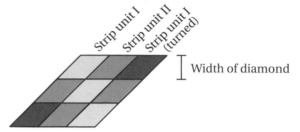

Measure the width of the small diamonds and add seam allowances to this dimension. Cut straight-of-grain strips this width to form a strip unit for each row.

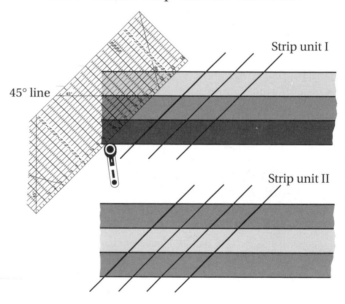

Cut strips width of small diamond + seam allowances. Make first cut at proper angle using ruler markings, in this case, 45°. Then, cut segments from strip units the width of small diamond + seam allowances.

Cut segments (finished size plus seam allowances) from each strip unit at an angle matching the type of diamond being made. For instance, to make a 60° diamond, cut the segments at a 60° angle using the 60° line on your ruler. It's a good idea to align the ruler-degree line with one of the inside seams, though, rather than the fabric edge. Sew the cut segments together to form the completed diamond.

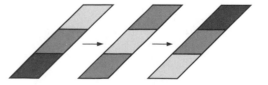

Analyzing Blocks For Rotary Cutting

Now that you have the basics of rotary cutting in mind, you will want to adapt other patterns to rotary cutting. Many books and patterns are written specifically for rotary techniques. Others have been adapted to rotary cutting, but it is helpful to know how to do it for your own designs. Here are a few examples of specific blocks that have been adapted to rotary cutting, step by step, to demonstrate the thinking behind the method. As you can see, each has two options for cutting the blocks. The option chosen depends on the number of blocks you want or your own personal preference.

SISTER'S CHOICE (10" BLOCK)

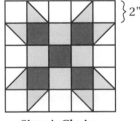

Sister's Choice

Block description: This block is a 10" square consisting of 5 equal-sized patches across and down. Thus, each finished patch measures 2" square.

Option I: Simple Cutting

Shapes needed:

1. Cut simple 2½" squares (2" finished size plus ½" for seam allowances).
2. Cut half-square triangles from 2⅞" squares (2" finished size plus ⅞").

Option II: Straight-of-Grain and Bias Strip Piecing

Shapes needed:

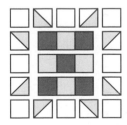

1. Use straight-of-grain strip piecing to assemble the Ninepatch unit in the center of the block. Cut strips 2½" wide (2" finished size plus ½" for seam allowances). See "Straight-of-Grain Strip Piecing" on pages 23–24.
2. Cut eight single 2½" squares for the block's corner squares and sides.
3. Cut bias-square units instead of half-square triangles. Cut bias strips 2½" wide for simple strip units or 2¾" wide for multiple bias strip units. See "Bias Strip Piecing" on pages 29–32.

CRAZY ANN (10" BLOCK)

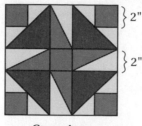
} 2"

} 2" Block description: This 10" block has 4" pieced corner squares composed of two sizes of half-square triangles and a 2" square. The center sashings are 2" x 4" pieced rectangles with a 2" center square.

Crazy Ann

Option I: Simple Cutting

Shapes needed:

1. Use simple cutting techniques to cut four 2½" corner squares and one 2½" center sashing square.
2. Use simple cutting techniques to cut the large 4" half-square triangles from 4⅞" squares (4" + ⅞"). Cut the small 2" half-square triangles from 2⅞" squares (2" + ⅞"). See cutting "Half-Square Triangles" on page 13.
3. Cut the 2" x 4" half-rectangles from 2⅝" x 5¼" rectangles. See cutting "Half-Rectangles" on page 15.

Option II: Strip Piecing

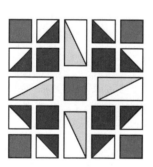

Shapes needed:

1. Use simple cutting techniques to cut eight 2½" corner squares and one 2½" center sashing square.
2. Cut eight 2½" bias squares. Use 2½"-wide bias strips for simple bias strip units or 2¾"-wide bias strips for multiple bias strip units. See "Bias Strip Piecing" on pages 29–32.
3. Cut pieced rectangles from 2½"-wide off-bias strips, using the BiRangle™ ruler or a paper cutting guide. See cutting "Strip-Pieced Rectangles" on pages 41–42.

STAR OF THE EAST (10 ¼" BLOCK)

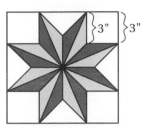

Star of the East

Block description: This block is composed of eight 45° pieced diamonds with 3" corner squares. The diamond legs are 3" long.

Option I: Simple Cutting

Shapes needed:

1. Cut the 3½" corner squares using simple cutting techniques.
2. Cut the set-in triangles as quarter-square triangles so that the long edges are on the straight of grain. Measure the long edge. In this case, it is 4¼", but if it is an odd size, round it up to the nearest ⅛". Cut a square 1¼" larger than the long edge. In this case, 4 ¼" + 1¼" = 5½". Cut one square for every four triangles needed. Trim the outer edge to size after it is sewn in place. See cutting "Quarter-Square Triangles" on pages 13–14.
3. Cut the half-diamonds from straight-of-grain strips of fabric that are the width of the half-diamond including its seam allowances. Make a paper cutting guide of the half-diamond and cut as many half-diamonds as you need from the fabric strips. See "Paper Cutting Guides" on page 18.

Option II: Strip Piecing

Shapes needed:

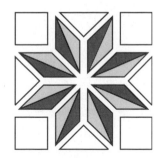

1. Same as Option I.
2. Same as Option I.
3. Cut simple strip-pieced half-diamonds from seamed strips of fabric, using a half-diamond paper cutting guide. Cut the strips the width of the half-diamond including seam allowances. Seam the strips together on both raw edges. Using a half-diamond paper cutting guide, cut the half-diamonds from the seamed strips. See cutting "Simple Strip-Pieced Half-Diamonds" on page 44.

CASTLES IN THE AIR (10" BLOCK)

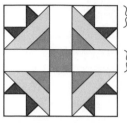

}2"

}2" Block description: When drafted, each pieced corner unit is 4" square and is composed of a square, two sizes of triangles, and a trapezoid. The four rectangles are 2" x 4" and the center square is 2" square.

Castles in the Air

Option I: Simple Cutting

Shapes needed:

1. Use simple cutting techniques to cut the 2½" (2" finished) squares and 2½" x 4½" (2" x 4" finished) rectangles.
2. The small triangles require the straight of grain to be on the long edge and, therefore, should be cut as quarter-square triangles. The long edge of this triangle is one-half the finished size of the pieced corner square (4") and, thus, measures 2". To cut quarter-square triangles this size from a square, add 1¼" and cut a square this size (3¼") for every four triangles needed. See cutting "Quarter-Square Triangles" on page 13.
3. The larger triangles are half-square triangles since they require the straight of grain on the short edges. They are cut from squares ⅞" larger than the finished size of the short leg, which is also 2". Cut one 2⅞" square for every two triangles needed. See cutting "Half-Square Triangles" on page 13.
4. To cut the trapezoids, use one of the following methods:
   a. Cut the trapezoids from bias strips of fabric ½" wider than the trapezoid, using a paper cutting guide. Use bias strips so the outer edge of the trapezoid is on the straight of grain. See "Paper Cutting Guides" on page 18.

   OR

   b. Cut the trapezoids by modifying right triangles. Cut two 4⅞" squares into four half-square triangles. Remove corners, using a paper cutting guide of the trapezoid, including seam allowances. See "Modifying Shapes" on page 19.

Option II: Strip Piecing

Shapes needed:

1. Cut simple squares for the corner squares.
2. To make the center block sashings, use one of the following methods:
   a. Cut a simple 2½" square and four 2½" x 4½" rectangles for the center block sashings.

   OR

   b. Strip-piece part of the center block sashing if there are a number of blocks to construct. Cut strips ½" wider than the finished width of the shapes, then seam and cut into segments ½" longer than the desired length. See "Straight-of-Grain Strip Piecing" on page 23.
3. Cut side-by-sides from 2⅞" bias squares (2" finished size plus ⅞"). See "Side-by-Sides" on page 34. Cut bias strips the width of the bias squares or ¼" wider for multiple strip units.
4. Cut center-striped half-square triangles from striped squares. Cut the corner bias strip ⅝" wider than the finished width of the triangle. Cut the center bias strip 1" wider than double the width of the trapezoid since this strip will be cut in half through its middle. Cut bias squares from the strip unit ⅞" wider than the finished size of the triangle's short edge (4" + ⅞" = 4⅞" bias squares). See cutting "Center-Striped, Half-Square Triangles" on page 38.

If you set aside some time to practice the rotary cutting techniques presented in *Shortcuts*, it will be easy to use them with your own creative ideas and applications. Make it a practice to look for the rotary-cutting potential in every design you see, whether traditional or original, using the section on analyzing blocks to help you adapt it to rotary cutting. With a little imagination and experimentation, you're sure to discover some shortcuts of your own.

That Patchwork Place Publications and Products

BOOKS

Angle Antics by Mary Hickey
Animas Quilts by Jackie Robinson
Appliqué Borders: An Added Grace by Jeana Kimball
Back to Square One by Nancy J. Martin
Baltimore Bouquets by Mimi Dietrich
Basket Garden by Mary Hickey
Blockbuster Quilts by Margaret J. Miller
Calendar Quilts by Joan Hanson
Cathedral Window: A Fresh Look by Nancy J. Martin
Corners in the Cabin by Paulette Peters
Country Threads by Connie Tesene and Mary Tendall
Even More by Trudie Hughes
Fantasy Flowers: Pieced Flowers for Quilters
    by Doreen Cronkite Burbank
Feathered Star Sampler by Marsha McCloskey
Fit To Be Tied by Judy Hopkins
Five- and Seven-Patch Blocks & Quilts for the ScrapSaver™
    by Judy Hopkins
Four-Patch Blocks & Quilts for the ScrapSaver™
    by Judy Hopkins
Go Wild with Quilts: 14 North American Birds and Animals
    by Margaret Rolfe
Handmade Quilts by Mimi Dietrich
Happy Endings—Finishing the Edges of Your Quilt
    by Mimi Dietrich
Holiday Happenings by Christal Carter
Home for Christmas by Nancy J. Martin and Sharon Stanley
In The Beginning by Sharon Evans Yenter
Jacket Jazz by Judy Murrah
Lessons in Machine Piecing by Marsha McCloskey
Little By Little: Quilts in Miniature by Mary Hickey
Little Quilts by Alice Berg, Sylvia Johnson, and
    Mary Ellen Von Holt
Lively Little Logs by Donna McConnell
Loving Stitches: A Guide to Fine Hand Quilting
    by Jeana Kimball
More Template-Free™ *Quiltmaking* by Trudie Hughes
Nifty Ninepatches by Carolann M. Palmer
Nine-Patch Blocks & Quilts for the ScrapSaver™
    by Judy Hopkins
Not Just Quilts by Jo Parrott
On to Square Two by Marsha McCloskey
Osage County Quilt Factory by Virginia Robertson
Painless Borders by Sally Schneider
A Perfect Match: A Guide to Precise Machine Piecing
    by Donna Lynn Thomas
Picture Perfect Patchwork by Naomi Norman
Piecemakers® *Country Store* by the Piecemakers
Pineapple Passion by Nancy Smith and Lynda Milligan
A Pioneer Doll and Her Quilts by Mary Hickey

Pioneer Storybook Quilts by Mary Hickey
*Quick & Easy Quiltmaking: 26 Projects Featuring Speedy
    Cutting and Piecing Methods* by Mary Hickey,
    Nancy J. Martin, Marsha McCloskey & Sara Nephew
Quilts for All Seasons: Year-Round Log Cabin Designs
    by Christal Carter
Quilts for Kids by Carolann M. Palmer
Quilts from Nature by Joan Colvin
Quilts to Share by Janet Kime
Red and Green: An Appliqué Tradition by Jeana Kimball
Red Wagon Originals by Gerry Kimmel and Linda Brannock
Rotary Riot: 40 Fast and Fabulous Quilts by Judy Hopkins
    and Nancy J. Martin
Scrap Happy by Sally Schneider
*Sensational Settings: Over 80 Ways to Arrange Your Quilt
    Blocks* by Joan Hanson
Sewing on the Line: Fast and Easy Foundation Piecing
    by Lesly-Claire Greenberg
Shortcuts: A Concise Guide to Rotary Cutting
    by Donna Lynn Thomas (metric version available)
Small Talk by Donna Lynn Thomas
Smoothstitch™ *Quilts: Easy Machine Appliqué*
    by Roxi Eppler
The Stitchin' Post by Jean Wells and Lawry Thorn
Strips That Sizzle by Margaret J. Miller
Tea Party Time: Romantic Quilts and Tasty Tidbits
    by Nancy J. Martin
Template-Free™ *Quiltmaking* by Trudie Hughes
Template-Free™ *Quilts and Borders* by Trudie Hughes
Template-Free® *Stars* by Jo Parrott
Watercolor Quilts by Pat Maixner Magaret and
    Donna Ingram Slusser
Women and Their Quilts by Nancyann Johanson Twelker

TOOLS

6" Bias Square®	Rotary Mate™
8" Bias Square®	Rotary Rule™
Metric Bias Square®	Ruby Beholder™
BiRangle™	ScrapSaver™
Pineapple Rule	

VIDEO

Shortcuts to America's Best-Loved Quilts

Many titles are available at your local quilt shop. For more information, send $2 for a color catalog to That Patchwork Place, Inc., PO Box 118, Bothell WA 98041-0118 USA.

☎ Call 1-800-426-3126 for the name and location of the quilt shop nearest you.